T5-CVC-260

Raspberrying

for
Victor, Lora, Waldo,
Ronald, Alvin, Carol,

& those
who raspberried with us

# Raspberrying

## By Leonard Neufeldt

Black Moss Press

© 1991 by Leonard Neufeldt

Published by Black Moss Press
P.O. Box 143, Station A, Windsor, Ontario N9A 6L7

Black Moss books are distributed in Canada and the United States by
Firefly Books, Ltd., 250 Sparks Ave., Willowdale, Ontario M2H 2S4

Financial assistance towards publication of this book
was gratefully received from the Canada Council
and the Ontario Arts Council.

Cover art by Sarita Baker and John Fraser.
Author photo courtesy of Purdue University.

Versions of poems in this collection have appeared in the following:
*Chariton Review, Descant, Madrona, Malahat Review,*
*Mennonite Mirror, Prairie Fire,* and *Sycamore Review.*

Canadian Cataloguing in Publication Data

Neufeldt, Leonard, 1937-
  Raspberrying

Poems.
ISBN 0-88753-222-5


  I. Title.

PS8577.E758R38 1991   C811'.54   C91-090196-1
PR9199.3.N48R38 1991

# Contents

## The Angel at the Gate

He calls it Yarrow.
North of the past.
It's not here, and not the river
whose rings of light we watched
in morning rain:
Scottish hills whitened
with flowers like sheep on the other side
and along the road and stone wall and fences —
the same name for flower, river, and town
of river stone, stucco, and small windows.

It's somewhere, she says, touching his closed eyes
with the gently roughened fingertip
of a healer, and he feels again
the faintest color red.
Tell me what you see.

"I see them setting tables, many tables,
covered with white,
and someone looking away
to the mountains. His hand opens like a flower
but more slowly, coaxing out fire.
Mountains turn transparent; people
shade their eyes against the evening sun."

## The Upper Chilliwack River

It's easier to reach by the Chilliwack Lake Road,
enmeshed suddenly in light
where it twists out of shade, and back in,
bringing angular trees, time, half-familiar place
too close to dustlines on the windshield,
ready to answer questions head-on.
Or there; come by the shore, carefully:
the rockslope slides to the water and is gone,
foam shifts in the pool
and leaves fan out with the foam, with room to tack
round and round where the current slides
toward the shore under the buttonbushes,

and out again, to the middle.  Leaves on edge,
converging, running to the Fraser Valley,
the Vedder River, the Canal,
vanishing downstream like berry seasons,
pickers, Co-op trucks, box factory,
canneries one by one, the chinaman,
young women, Dyke View Berry Farm.
You are left to shift feet against
the water-slick tilt of rock,
against wetness of leaves in the mind,
and something remembered, something you have known
swaled to move more quickly
swept away
rushing ahead of bursts of water
at the start of the next cascade.

In the greenest pool of the river
leaves swirl away
among clouds lurching steadily eastward,
dizzying. A last cloud gathers remaining leaves
and gives itself downstream.
The pool deepens
to the stillness of the speckled trout
all in motion, his eye looking upstream,
tail stalking instincts through lines of light
converging below him.
Leaf shadows drift across his fin and flank,
and foam closes over.

# Dyke View Berry Farm

## 1.

Time couldn't take away our words but place changed them.
Words are a family trait.  Our Mennonite ancestors —
teachers, traders, poets, garrulous
farmers, businessmen, brandymakers, musicians —
were mostly too poor or too suddenly rich
to stop talking, and everyone was spoken for
before he was born.  Strange idioms
in a land as foreign as the Fraser Valley
made little difference.  Father, a businessman
who studied music and dreamed of teaching choirs
that sang only pianissimo
learned silence on his own
but it made no dent on his children,
and it didn't change the fact that in 1619
his tirelessly non-resistant Dutch forebears
forsook salt marshes, canals, dykes, orchards
and waist-high grasses to do their talking,
singing, and praying out loud in Schleswig
while the Spanish armies broke the truce
and then the dykes and for the greater glory of God
gutted quivering fields and those
who stayed because they could not leave
or praising God too generously left too late.

2.

The year that Father kept everything to himself
he bought six open acres of hard bottom land
where the lower Chilliwack River, renamed the Vedder
and redirected, received the upper Chilliwack
from a high mountain valley and spilled into Sumas Lake.
Canada geese gathered like immigrants
to gabble by thousands among themselves
over water rights while the Fraser Valley
was subdivided from Yarrow, before it had a name,
to the northside wall of mountains the shade of blueprints
engineers had drawn of the Canal, the dykes
on either side gray lines, straight as raspberry rows.


3.

As our raspberry rows blossomed with a hum of bees
winter died eastward, mountain to mountain,
and the new President of the Yarrow Co-op
announced price hikes, a larger cannery,
and six tons per acre, crops palpable as geese
returning by thousands along the Vedder Canal
from the States, where the fresh-painted Co-op trucks
would soon again deliver twice a week
coopered whiskey barrels that leaked raspberry jam
down Highway 11 past the U.S.
Customs officers who waved them on excessively.

4.

Why ancestors left Holland was as important
to Father as history planted here and now
in rows, if possible, in soil one's bones claim as their own,
paid for before its yield is known, hard
as the clay of Dyke View Berry Farm.
The dyke silvering north and south
for miles of old lake bottom when the fog
rolled free of poplars and Vedder Mountain
and the sun; the earth hardening
to a gray slate before it turned grass green.


5.

Grasses grew everywhere in our berry rows,
sprouting, we swore, from the canes themselves.
We warred against wild grasses: five brothers,
hoes thudding like pheasants startled
from their nests, hoes made by our blacksmith,
Mr. Reimer, whose arms were hard as anvils,
who didn't know how hard our soil was because
Father didn't explain why he wanted heavy
blades made, and he never held a hoe
except to match handle to son. Our hoes bounced
with surprise as we argued with them,
as they sheared grasses that would grow again
and sometimes a berry plant that wouldn't;
sometimes the hoe wedged down to harder bottom,
a rock where it shouldn't have been,
and the back stiffened to say
"something too large to move,
something to build on."

6.

In our berry field Father wanted everything
to speak for itself: family name,
reclaimed lake and marshes, hardpan clay,
hymns chosen for Sunday, bumper crops,
another window broken in the pickers' cabins,
the unexpected death of the King,
pacifism, newly forged hoes.
Father, you rode your red tractor
through our shouts across the rows, our hoes,
backs, arms, and thin buttocks held tight
against wires and plants to let you by
singing Mendelssohn's *Elijah*, your left hand
conducting dustpan rows, your right
feeling the jabs of the wheel.
Only into the second chorus, your favorite, you drove
into the drainage canal: tractor — cultivator — harrow —
conductor's score. "No boys, the clutch failed."
You shook your trouser legs and music. We bent
to our work, begged the hard earth to bear us out
as we reached inward, dreaming of crop failures,
hungry for anything but raspberries.

# Handbook for Berrypickers

I

If you have never picked raspberries
the sky will awaken with purple, then
mountains south and north, then the sun.
Blue insouciance will walk through mists
on the valley floor for another hour.
If you have travelled far to pick for five or six weeks
don't be afraid.

The picking season begins
with the power of voices
in dying shadows. Laughter of pure color,
ghostly protests making endposts bold
with jackets and yellow straw hats,
two divebombing killdeer protecting nests unseen,
unguarded songs warming the sun
and the wires of the rows,
lightly stained fingers baring shoulders
one at a time, slowly as a confession,
a shout small as a bird from a distant field,
the unfathomably soft ambush
of a spider's thread of light, transparent
across the row to bring you to yourself,
to the burning where a new vine,
next year's stock, found a way
outside the wires overnight, again,
and like a nail hidden in the endpost etched the back
of your hand and wrist and arm and upper arm,
and for a moment you want to back away
forever, to breathe where the valley vanishes
to the west.

14

The day will bring your life
this far, will lose it nearer the light,
will attach what remains of you
to the hard earth underfoot,
the blond new berry stand with its dusty feet,
and bushes triumphant with red
of ripened raspberries.


II

If this is not your first season
you will have stood against the rain before,
breast to breast with mostly unpicked
berry bushes and wondered what you should do
because the day's obscure account of you
began when it was drenched by the first drop of rain,
and your eyes wanted to close
until the horizon changed but they watched
the leaves change and left you utterly alone.
This time you will let your fingers whiten
like the skin-smooth stem-end piths
where you've already picked.
Your nuckles will nudge higher your straw hat
swelling heavy with rain
and rub numbness from your forehead
as water beads and hangs like berries
from upper and lower wires and leaf tips.

If the clouds press eastward to the upper valley
and rise to brush Mount Lady
you'll find larger berries
inside plants of inside rows, berries still wet,
ready to fall when the smell of wetness

has gone.  When you carry the next full flat
wet against your thighs to the weighhouse
the last mountain will float out of smoky clouds
somewhere between your desire to quit and the light
sticking once again to acres of raspberry leaves.

Largest berries do not grow in the light.
They grow closer to the mountains
than to Dyke View Berry Farm.
You'll have heard about them:  cedar-green silence,
fields free of arguments and desire,
each berry beautiful beyond description,
but tasteless.  Their flavor is nothing
compared to smaller berries you have picked
all morning in the rain, and which you have brought
to the weighhouse, where people you know
were expecting you.

## Garter Snakes

Because Betty Wedel walked the shimmering rows
upright as a hallelujah the wind
searched undersides of leaves
and turned them to the sun.
Because she bent arch-backed
from her hips to the ground
for berries overripe and overlooked
in the last picking
we bent low over our pickers' stands
of filled and half-filled flats.
We sent our best berries from hiding,
aim surer than the messages
we wanted to be found out
but only half understood —
splattered leaves and red splattered ears
bending us still lower —
until a sudden snake would straighten us
by darting leaflike down the bush
we'd been picking and twisting away
to June Watson in the next row
to catch the light between her brown sandalled feet
before we could catch it by the tail.
When her screams straightened 62 berry rows,
poplars, dyke, rim of mountains
and found her in the center of the Valley

17

she asked me if her older sister
had screamed that way when she taught us
second grade. I lied,
leaning on the cedar post between us,
and felt the strange happiness
of a small natural disaster, the same happiness
I had felt after my brother and I lied
to Betty Wedel when she wanted to know
who had tried to lift the back of her dress.

Our cousin couldn't lie when Betty
gaped at us, unable to scream,
whitened her eyes, stared past everything,
and thumped down on her back,
the fingers of her right hand fluttering
like leaves until a pailful of water
from the drainage canal brought her halfway
home to remembering, spluttering.
She closed her eyes, not wanting to know
that one of us had dropped
a frantic garter snake
into the wind-filled back of her blouse.

## Father was Known as a Man in Control

Conducting *a capella* choirs without perfect pitch
was a theological problem to Father
since he expected uncertainty in most things,
even berry prices.
Substitute umpire at home games,
he called all baserunners safe,
benefit of doubt forcing him to dodge
Seven-Up bottles and loose change
after he called a game because of dark
and overtired eyes, his balls and strikes
inaudible to batters, who stared past him
to the glow of a ridgelong forest fire
that surged and fell behind Vedder Mountain.

Who was to tell whether scoresheets,
eight-part motets, or berry price calls,
even if we had gotten any of them straight
as our miles of wires pulled tight
through new cedar posts to make rows,
proved anything to Father, who came home
earlier than usual
from a season-opening afternoon ballgame
with his nose broken in three places.

He hated to see things broken,
flimsy pickers' stands, doorlocks in the cabins,
hoe handles, an ivory baton we had given him
for his birthday, baseball bats,
windows — especially house windows
when he and Mother shopped in Vancouver

after the berries had peaked and they gave us
the day off. Rain forced our baseball game
inside, into the diningroom. We called
the game on account of broken windows.

Shopping in the city and replacing windows
made Father sure of how to deal with us,
at least for the evening as clouds deserted the sky
in the west and everything converged
on a speckled fledgling my older brother found
beading water, wing bent like a book,
balancing open-mouthed on its stomach
under the rainbows of the sprinkler
that had been turning all day.

## Mr. Ediger

Tall-stemmed Volksdeutscher   Wheat farmer with his father in a
Ukraine collective because Stalin closed the borders in 1929   A year
after German troop carriers arrived he carried back to his fatherland
love of honor, uniforms, overweight guard dogs, and rereading a few
pages each night like Hitler, whose white lips caressed running titles
page after page of *Der Deutsche Mensch* in his final bunkered weeks
beneath Berlin when the Russians caught up with Mr. Ediger   They
freed him a few years later to leave with wife for Canada and catch the
Canadian National Railroad west   Father hired him in May to help
hoe our berries because the soil was harder than ever   We were taking
violin lessons and playing in the orchestra with blistered hands.

With the war over Royal Canadian Air Force flyers showed their
stuff P51s in dogfights overhead, and they bombed the dyke with sacks
of flour   Mr. Ediger shook his hoe like a sword, not at the planes per
se but as if to cut off shouts and fingers so that he could probe further
the politics of our parents "Hitler was a great man, a simple man who

did his best, and all the rest is Jewish propaganda — the only Jews who died deserved to" And we boys mortared him with granite-hard clods of earth when he wasn't looking wishing that the incoming were 100-pound sacks of flour — Maple Leaf — northern hard wheat — number one grade to whiten his Aryanism and pathogenetic eyes He wife wailed at Mustangs snap-rolling out of the sun's rings and screaming down through treetops, packed her son and screamed her lower-pitched way to the outhouse, a two holer, to protect her child from the Allied raids.

Bombs of white blossomed among poplars lining the dyke as our peaceable father received our reports without a word He surveyed the battle on all sides from the saddle of his coughing Massey-Harris tractor stepped down stiff-backed to his heels walked head down in step with us and berry cane in hand and sacked him.

## Sunday Services

In the half-dark balcony
that grew in rows toward the light
of windows flanking the pulpit parapet
of the massive Yarrow Mennonite Brethren Church,
berry-red hands of ushers picked the ripest
and rowdiest on the men's side
and left the rest of us for other harvests
as the choir and Father in white
mused in unsteady lines of light.

    *Sweet sabbath morning*
      *all life adorning*
windows singing. Widows nodded,
pickers said maybe, fingers felt wire,
sleeves said no, vines said wait.
*Oh may thy peace in our hearts abide…*

and the pheasant's four white-bleaching eggs
that made midsummer a matter of wings
from the berry field to the flank of dyke
    'she will not return
    she will not return.'

# Mother

i

Charlie Fong, you must have been as white
to them as the rice you bought on credit
with vegetables and tea.  Some
called you Funk, wrote your name the same
as the lecherously gentle, blue-eyed grocer
who kept a separate book on you,
and by the office door told you
of land you could rent for nothing,
plant raspberries, join the Co-op,
and walk to services with the rest of us,
and not just for weddings, festivals, and funerals,
when a thousand or more would eat in three shifts.

You showed them, stooping forward more and more
like a Buddhist monk and growing potatoes
on land leased from Mrs. Riesen
after her husband was buried and everyone joined
the family in the meal of remembrance.
"Hundred-fifty-foursack" you counted for me
where we sat on the last row, next to my parents' orchard
and you rose slowly and righted a sack
that had toppled, spilling red potatoes, many eyes,
the largest potatoes I had ever seen.
I knew it was all in the way you had dug them up

while the sun slipped behind the lattice-work
of Mr. Froese's raspberry vines. "No soon," you said
and told me of your children north of Canton,
where they had moved because of the war.
You dropped every "r," endings, words, you separated
sentences like children's names, like potatoes
you had not wanted to spear with the fork
in digging them up,
and you took them with you, the damaged ones,
for your bachelor's pantry and homebrew.
I imagined your children, some of them called Funk,
and a war beyond a dark forest
and wide river, and on the other side
of a mountain too high for you or me to climb.


ii


At bedtime, when Mother came to find me,
the two of you talked like father and mother,
though Father never sounded Chinese, as she did
that evening, dropping endings and words
and speaking too fast for me to understand,
diaspora of sentences, dialect of the displaced.
We shivered among potato sacks
that turned to stone soldiers,
and the night rose around us temple-like
under a star that wanted to come closer.

In the window by my bed there were no stars
when the light was on, but in the glass
I could see Mother on the other side,
which was darker than here where she prayed,
warily in perfect English, her fingers berry-stained

and her almighty Watchman of Jerusalem's Broken Walls
smiling in the back of her pale green
Klippenstein eyes, where He'd better listen to her,
immune to Co-op statistics and red potatoes.
He could shape a new world out of
falling prices, raspberry fields,
clay harder than jute sacks of new potatoes,
and all the dispossessed from Adam
to Yarrow, British Columbia, and you, Charlie Funk,
and her children, children's children
walking up sabbath-ripe rows, raspberrying.

## The Joyless Don't Know Everything

Even the retired preachers got out of bed
by five-thirty or so in the morning.
Not a word about the Old Country
or berry flats stacked too high
at the rear of Co-op trucks,
which had lurched forward again
and sent stacks of filled flats
from the truckbed down
to the gray gravel reddening.  No aspersions.
When folks of our raspberry town were told
they'd have a chance to visit God
in a place of their choice
they said *here*.

So did pickers imported
from Saskatoon and Swift Current,
who only yesterday had asked
if any in Yarrow had ever sat
at the same table with a famous person.

But two broad-hipped, white gloved women
in patent leather pumps
and Grandmother in royal blue
with white flowers on her widebrimmed hat
confided to God upon closing the door
and lowering their voices
that our berry growing was done in jest.

## Tubing on the Vedder After Picking

"A woman is a woman, boys, and this river
has the right shape.  Too young to know
what I mean, but you'll know her ways better
when your skin is cold all over
and you brace your bones to climb the shore
miles downstream."

The river silver-tongued
whispering to each of us, each his name.
Veins of shoreline reaching out,
carrying the river, holding the evening light,
felt in the body feeling the soundless erosion
of all things, and a gull lifted away
too suddenly, screaming:

three boys on a high dyke, shivering,
waiting for the dark.

# The Young Women of Yarrow

*for Lora and Carol*

In church young women
kept their sleeves down and mouths shut
and smiled if older women bulking the entrance
with simple hats and pins and uncut hair
nodded and let them by to be ushered
early to their seats in the front, on the left side —
except for Grandmother, women's usher,
who weeklong wore the cap
of midwife and nurse and Sundays
hats large as the Queen Mum's in the *Vancouver Sun*:
bosswoman. She waved bitter-smiling young women
to their place as though they had started into labor,
and the few who hurriedly found
their own seats far back she reseated
as though she was burying them.

Those women talked and picked faster
in the fields than young men, much faster
than the men who rechecked rows picked clean
by the women, blouses loosened
at the top and sleeves pushed up by mid-morning.
They carried their own berry-soaked flats
to the weighhouse, lifted them to the top
of the stack, waited for the flats to stop swaying
before returning to the row.
Some would grow strong like those who had left.
She put on a new dress to visit
the women in the field.

One day they would stop breaking their backs;
one day they would leave the starch out
of their fathers' collars, but not her husband's shirts,
not her daughters. Her granddaughters were strong;
they wheedled her daughters,
choosing hymns for their own weddings,
and they would find their own seats
on the right side with their children.
Some of the granddaughters climbed with their men
for almost a day to the top of Mount Cheam
to see the Pacific
separate itself left and right,
slowly, from the slate-green sky
a hundred miles away.

## Box Factory Girls

Girls in bridal white blouses
walking to Guenther's box factory
when Bible School had closed
and azaleas opened like swans.
Bees hadn't yet roused berry fields
and no one else was hiring.
Not even guys with hopped-up cars
and open-throttle exaggerations
knew much about the box factory girls.

Inside the front door the girls exchanged
the fragrance of early morning muskrat grass
for the sweet astringency of freshly cut wood.
They stopped to watch two men,
nails in their teeth and brains, cobble raspberry flats,
side and bottom slats to grooved ends with shingle nails,
two hammer strokes per nail and taped fingers,
and then the crooning scream of the mill saw next door.

Below the loft to the right of the door
darkness stayed the whole day.  Above the loft
light spilled through skylight windows
and wide cracks around them, and gathered flecks
of dust into lines that bent the loft's two-by-four
railing.  Sandals clacking at the heels,
they mounted the ladder rungs
and held the second last one, looked up
as though to find a sunspot floating in the eye.

And then, at the top, their blouses caught
the light. They tied their hair up,
sat down straight-backed,
napes stretched, arms forward,
before chest-high cast-iron staplers,
heads ready to bob like pianists.
Three percussive notes: dismissively
they flung the box into the cage below,
a pint box of two pieces
stapled and tossed in a single motion.

The young man who started work before the girls
and lowered his eyes before they climbed the ladder,
sometimes every second rung,
increased the pace of his two-handed jamming,
six boxes at a time — hollocks we called them —
twice into each flat. He stacked flats
with fresh hollocks shiny as sap,
soon to be spotted with red stains
of the first picking.

As summer came on, another stapler was hired.
Fingers and pedal feet grew more desperate.
When the girls' eyes met,
heads would stop bobbing,
and they nodded sidelong to each other,
laughing soundlessly, keeping their secrets
in the loft till the dark rose from beneath
to disconnect their machines. They climbed
the ladder down, their feet slightly spread.

If the guys with cars stood in the doorway
or stepped inside to watch the girls descend

one after the other, the girls looked
at each other, retied their hair,
and knew exactly where to step in the dark
to leave through another door
and walk together on the cedar sidewalk
of Yarrow Central Road, past vague shapes
of church and Co-op store and school,
toward the coming season.

Always they had their work cut out for them,
one day fastened to the next in quick succession,
tossed down to be assembled in larger frames
freshly numbered:  love, double weddings
under twin arches, still-births, many children,
parents sometimes senile, sometimes lucid
and wanting to die but saying so only to each other
and their daughters.  Memories of hard work,
four-foot stapler machines accompanying
the imagined, and the cage
full to the top with boxes by nightfall;
in the morning thinking of what will be,
walking a mile and more down Central Road
on the moss-bordered wooden walk,
picking white Yarrow flowers, flinging them aside
like raspberry boxes before they reached the door.

They'd look up the ladder where staplers waited,
where shiny slats were turned into boxes
and shadows into wind and hair into leaves
shivering against stems
when morning seeps like cold canal water
through berry rows and grows large as the field.
And their sandalled feet
counted the steps of the ladder again.

# Grandfather

His clothes are baggy, weighted with sphagnum,
fungi eat at his trouser cuffs,
lichens have blotched the nubs of his fingers,
and algae drift in the corner of his eyes.
He is busy with a field of cedar posts
fourteen to a row, shaking them rudely
awake before he tightens the wires,
replacing upper wires he has snapped
in trying to get too much out of them,
wresting the last of his strength from them,
winching it around endposts
as though to cut clean through.

"Ten children went before in death
and four grandchildren."
He remembered them like row numbers. "Children
are gifts from God," he had said
at a grandson's burial, but they were names,
orphans sleeping inside him
like maps of another country yellowing
in a foreign language,
names separating at the foldlines.

He accounted for each of us, the living,
by forgetting our names, and then he forgot
the road out of town to our berry farm, Dyke Road,
and names of children who had died.
We tightened wires and tested posts alone,
shook them gently in the long aisles,
replaced with fewer words the far too many
broken, held up by sagging wires.

# The Mole

I dig down for the rotted endpost base
and a finger writes from inside
the earth, light
glinting blades of couchgrass
something has made to stand on end,
sudden shape without sound
moving like a word in the margin
toward its new life,
searching its own darkness for direction,
humping the world in a thin line:
silence plowing past blossoming berry plants,
almost touching the feet,
outwaiting treachery above

as though being here mattered.
Hands twist the blond handle
of a carbon blue spade
new as its own dull twang;
and snow begins to flake slowly down
from out a sudden cloud of seeds, arms,
legs, eyes — the airy distinctness melting
as it touches plowed earth between the rows.
I bend down to find where the moving line
began, where it burrows,
searching for signs that won't arrive,
trying to get them under thumb
already departed, vanished,
a raspberry field in their wake.
No legend blackened roots,
no collapse, no edges turned up
to silver softly in the sun when it returns.
But under the knee, damp, aching,
earth is giving way.

## The Cannery Manager, Mr. Penner

This cannery accepts rain, the loss
of another week of picking, processing, shipping.
Losses are set by what to expect.
We accept mold on berries although I dock growers
moderately, I accept the poverty of leaves,
the sacrifice of a season
and night and bed. When there is time
I sleep well.
All night the rain has no need of me,
which I forget without forgetting
raspberry leaves on the silver-wet lawn
by our garden,
how red they are for a morning when the rain relents.

This year has been no different except I know
how young our workers are and I can't forget
their petition: children born of blandishment
have come like exiles among us,
they would rather be wrong than not.
Their folly of writing the Labor Board
dried up overnight when I fired
the first three names, Dahl, Allert, Neufeldt,
three of the new crop,
apologetic as an hour of sun on Monday,
about to steal morale in this summer of rain,

and my secretary misspelled every word
in my report:
a typist useless as rubles
in those days when revolutionaries
and Czarist secret police in Russia
somehow assumed each other's names and places
and changed the name of the country
but not the harvest requisitions,
or drought, or hunger, or winter oats
for our one remaining horse, which we ate.

Few letters from America, and all of them
mentioning letters we hadn't received.
It was the lost letters we most wanted
to answer, and I planned to write our neighbor
who had left the year before that I was coming
too, but there was little paper.
We surprised him in the new world:
"so much worthless money!" we had brought
in a footlocker, to put away with his surprise
and the diary books we had bought
before leaving, but hadn't used.
When our salaries dropped we worked longer hours,
humming falsetto to ourselves alone,
pilgrim songs, until our ears rang,
the heart's secret, faint as the thunder roll
of Sinai, unmistakable,
calling for us to keep it company.

# Message by the Reverend Peter P. Neufeldt

*To the memory of Uncle Peter*

"I am sorry
for letting a broad river pass through my fingers
without drinking a single drop."
That's what a famous poet wrote.
Should anyone make his pain so imprecise,
yet here, this very moment
tempered with regret long after the fact?
I'm sorry for him too, unlike my nephew
who likes his work.
He wouldn't have wasted Old World piety
on the anniversary album of our congregation
making blurred black and white faces
at those of us here from the founding,
when we changed plans by the month
instead of mocking ourselves,
when we built this church together
since no one knew enough about building,
or loneliness.  Raspberries gave none of us privileges,
or plowing them under, or moving away.

We travelled lightly when we left the Old World;
we've travelled lightly in this Valley,
ready to protect whatever came with us:
the solitude of growing seasons,
exile, obedience, freedom, departure, song —
a note given to find our parts,
to sing together across the rows
the first stanza memorized, and sometimes more,
starting what we know, what our children will complete,
that part of ourselves that sings when the next page
is missing, when we're unsure
and watch each other for half-formed words.

You've seen the place below Vedder Crossing
where the river's main channel
cuts the cliff clean.
If we stopped there, if we let water pass
bitter-cold through our fingers before drinking,
and after drinking shook it slowly from our hands,
the river would turn from the rock-blue wall
to find a valley and the deep center of the Canal
running to the Fraser behind Sumas Mountain.

Some of you remember how our train westbound
stopped at the Great Divide. For a quarter hour
we left Bibles, footlockers, maps,
unattended. We mingled with non-immigrants
and with a strangeness that cut through the air
and our thin coats.
There, the cordillera of a new continent
separating a future from a past:
one milky stream numbing our hands and running
to three oceans. No one can see that far.
*Ich kenn einen Strom*— join me, please,
in this song. George Reimer will lead us —
*Ich kenn einen Strom dessen herrliche Flut*
*fliesst wunderbar stille durch's Land,*
countless ripples agitated from within,
familiar — where berries grow
and rivers run to seas.

## The '48 Flood

A river will tell downstream
what mountains won't:
gravity that draws down moments,
moils them among rocks, gasping mud,
splintered trees and roof of the new house
on the mountain road. Or the river draws water
clear enough to see grains of sand
fishtail downstream past spawning nests
until we feel safe with mountain
and river except when the river cannot stop
rising.

      A river turning free of mountains
will rebuild rippled sky and mountain
downward from the middle to the dark beneath,
where you want to step down breathless.
The river will send only itself, clear, disentangled,
to wash the midwife breathing hard for everyone,
babe red as berries, mother even if she doesn't
survive, sheets from the white closet shelf,
and the husband who sits outside holding
his mouth tightly shut because he has heard
the scream of a woman who doesn't want to die.

And the river will carry down the spirit
uprooted, eddying in the margin,
sleepless, shaking itself dry.

When the Vedder cannot stop rising
it uproots berry fields, two-room shacks
and corkscrew willows in the flood plain,
and they get it wrong again in the current.
It softens the heart of the dyke.  Young men
feel the desire to rush overtop
this one time, to break out
the other side.
Mothers past childbearing chide daughters
and pray indulgently for sons in the fields,
where postholes fill with water, where
legs feel the loss of feeling,
and drainage ditches collapse, covering the spade,
muddying the handle to the tip of the spine;
thinnest lungs feel themselves sought out.

The Vedder has filled the absence beneath us all,
seeping from field to berry field,
finding basements from below, filling them
with shimmering night, drowning
salamanders, spiders, stray cats,
the idiot daughter who looked older than her parents
by the time she learned to wash herself.

Douglas Fir rose straight as hour glasses. On the lower slopes cedars leaned toward the mountain road, brushing trucks that passed beneath in second gear — berries in summer, cords of firewood in the fall. In the fields below we sang of a heavenly home and, spades in hand, planted drooping raspberry starts every two feet. Where Wilson Road narrowed to cross the railroad track and circled back at the Post Office and rain-forest mountain, a baseball field was cropped and marked with sacks of lime and dog-leg foul poles.

Two months after the flood a bumper crop destroyed us, cutting price calls short. Girls cut their sleeves shorter and neck curls longer. When the Co-op's new-painted stairs failed safety inspection the evangelists came.

One came to town with yodelling twin daughters and curly-headed songleader fidgeting his hands and feet when he sat down. Their gestetner leaflets left fragments of words in our palms, the evangelist's name, "The Ninety and Nine," "Where is my Wandering Boy Tonight," and Bible passages, black and in reverse. In the public hall above the Co-op store they tried to woo bankrupt berry farmers into song. All the farmers could sing, in parts, without sheet music, but most had left the Co-op and some the Church;

twins and songleader sang alone, looking side- long to the evangelist.
"You say when one-third of you rebel there is at least a one-third
chance some-thing's wrong with the Co-op administration. Listen
Yarrowers: there's something far more wrong here. The Lord's work
isn't like going to Cultus Lake for a day or watching a ballgame. You
people are holding yourself back as you did your berries. All of you
caught fast in the testicles of sin." And the song leader: "tentacles,
brother, tentacles," and I in a chair that sagged sideways towards the
stair-case, remembering rocks and a waterlogged dinghy I saw on the
bottom of the lake at 40 feet, and the new playing field with blue
bleachers, ready for the playoffs. And the evangelist refused to
wilt.

We knew he would last a couple of days, like new umpires who made
too many bad calls near the end of the season. He and his daughters
would pick berries further down the Valley to pay the rent. They would
sing of a land fairer than morning, where mountains no longer touched
the sky, and return to Saskatchewan.

Yarrow Growers, British Columbia Senior A Champions. Playing
on Sunday. The Co-op building for sale.

## Antaeus

In Yarrow pickers could do as they wished
within limits:  tongue-tied lovers
or merely tongue-tied, but tasting
astringency at the roots of our tongues
when the Canal rose to the top of the dykes
and berry fields swept away
their emptiness.
How can Yarrow feel her juice
when loggers stay home a year at a time
and derelict kids burn vacant
pickers' cabins? PICK-YOUR-OWN
signs everywhere, and Yarrowers do;
and they watch Winnebagos snubnose into town
and out to spend a week or two at the lake.

What's left of the sign sags forward
like Carrots Klassen, vegetarian pioneer:
WELCOME TO YA . . . . the old preachers
can't remember.  Antaeus is weakening
and Verily Jantzen, monotone songleader
in Sunday school, has lost his grip.
Grocers have bought each others' stores,
still full of pity, but ashamed the feeling
doesn't exclude those stopping to shop,
who point at what they buy,
who ask how far Cultus Lake is,
and if visitors are also allowed
to pick their own.

Redness will vanish like visitors,
without a trace.
Antaeus is dying quietly, thank God,
and because absence doesn't mean much anymore
it will empty more of the fields.
Raspberries are ripped from the earth, roots
reaching outward for each other, for soil
clinging to them like something you see
in the heart before it gets out
and dies.

## Letters to a Friend who has Moved Back and Planted Berries

1.

Only the minister's black and brown Chevy
could roll his son over a fence
too high for deer, and into a field
of fender-high oats across the road
from our berry field.  And only this car
"had more nerve than Dick Tracy" the son explained
as he beat the bent roof like an untuned kettle drum,
scattering crows that had figured out
the fastest way back after the dust
had widened the air among the poplars
and sifted over the dyke.
We called him a stupid Indian.

2.

In the championships Henry Stewart, who really was
an Indian, lapped everyone in the mile
and then lapped one of the guys twice.
They pinned another five blue pendants with medals
big as the sun across his barrel chest,
and we cheered him all the way to Mercury Drug Store.
He had let his body harden and turn brown
and his hair sweat black in track and field.
He caught steelhead in the upper Vedder
with illegal roe and let them gulp the chill air
while they died.  He flunked math,
and right there on Main Street smeared his brow
with soot after the Mounties asked him
why he had bloodied the mouth of the local bully
who had waited for him again between the stores.

3.

At family gatherings kids ate second shift,
all of us talking at once, turning feet on edge
inside our shoes and bumping knees on table legs.
But one of our cousins was quiet
as though the air was startled.  He was smaller
than his many brothers and broad shouldered,
and his eyes were large and blue.
When he married the Chief's daughter she took the name
of Grace and drove him home from the wedding.
While berry fields smoked like forests
where broken cedar posts and old stalks and prunings
of next year's canes were brought by armloads
to the pyres, he tried to teach her to fish,
and told her of light on the water in the shape
of a young girl running.  But she read books,
redecorated the house, drove their children to school,
gathered their toys and smiles as she could,
took care of the berries by herself,
and made stuffed cabbage leaves and raspberry pies
on Saturday.  When he died she thanked us
for our love.  Near the end,
when he couldn't get out of bed alone,
he drummed the silence with his fingers,
and let his blue eyes hum down to the roots,
and in the evenings redden.
What he missed most was rain falling for days,
driving to work on logging roads through low places
filled with water, and trees reaching into clouds.

"I always wondered if running up trees 180 feet high
was for him.  He started as a whistle-punk,
but one evening he told of how he loved to top
and thin out Douglas Fir before he wedged
and timbered them.  I was glad he couldn't anymore;
it's dangerous work" — her eyes unsteady
as the tribal canoe she had tried to steer
to spangles of light in the Canal
when he had watched from the dyke as a boy.
"Our berry rows behind the house were blossoming
and we hadn't yet pruned and topped them.
Sometimes you do the simple things."
Sometimes you go back to them.

# The Rhetoric of Raspberries

Faults of our language include archaic words,
absurd metaphors, and inordinate epithets.
      Aristotle's *Rhetoric*


Raspberries are not pomegranate blossoms
nor similes dark as dried blood, nor epics
like September stems graying with dissipation
upward from the roots and mold-wet earth;
but only 2300 years later
was Aristotle Mennonite, or half-Mennonite,
and on to something that should have been clearer
from the first picking.

When the idea reddened
his fingertips, uncut nails, and lips
slightly apart, he could taste and eat
what was also in his hand held farther back
for focus: the same raspberries
planting seeds between his teeth,
berries eaten yet uneaten, perfectly clarified
like clouds become one with the mountain.

The holy land was as near as Athens
and no farther away than marble-white towns and shrines
northward, smoking languidly in the evening sun.
He couldn't imagine berries large and red

in the Galilean hills as in Macedonia,
on the high ground of Mrs. Judkins' farm
above the lobster bay in Stonington, Maine,
in Dyke View Berry Farm, or the Sun-Ripe
cannery.

At the cannery, he would have scooped slop weights
of berry mold into a Continental Can
27-pound pail, lock-lid of brass
that mirrors every finger drumming it between loads,
getting close to something he believed in
for a whole week of night shift,
and if he had let the golden canister draw evening suns
into itself under the juice-slick planks
of the cannery loading dock,
the lid would have exploded
when the wine had clarified — ready
to take on rules that empire builders,
poets on the make,
voluminous Aquinas, the cannery manager
and our German teacher minded.

Raspberry Tea


Almost everything looks older, darker
in historic Salem.  The apothecary
has restored its appearance, and sells
ash-gray raspberry tea by the quarter pound.
Witches brew raspberry tea
to dull the ache of notoriety
when the first rosehips have been plucked,
when night dew brushes knees with mint.
Morning women, bare-footed in long skirts,
imagine a fragrance greener than the old common
or the garden mint and darker than the sea
by the old wharves below the Custom House.

Sun-stewed horse dung blackens
Indiana raspberries below the slatted fence
where crows strut after you've measured
one pot of Hoosier tea per plant.
You step sideways through weeds and thickening
morning smell into the house
and tightly shut the door, more than enough
raspberry leaves in hand to add astringency
to your pale clear Salem tea.

Anyone not United Empire Loyalist
in the Fraser Valley knew how to make raspberry tea.
On Dominion Day fill three colanders
with small leaves corrugated green,

smallest light green berries, abstemiously
wrinkled blossoms, tendril-white stems.
Dry them for a week on cotton frames
like thin apple slices, and when others
have left in the morning to pick the far end
of the field, rub and rub the tea
between your hands until the freshness
of the air tears the day gently to pieces
smaller than tea leaves.
Stop your hands, raise them in prayer;
memory will open them
as black poplars shift in the wind
and the fragrance fades.

There are other secrets you need to tell,
loyalties you thought had gone.
The wind from the poplars winnows the tea,
someone waits by a berry row
holding a morning darkness in closed hands.
You too have been used, surprised by grief —
you stoop to gather what you must.

Rooting

If I, a walker, arrive later than usual,
Clumsy with sciatica and weak eyes,
At our dacha, we call it, and flower and fruit gardens,
It's to find from you a way of walking,
Tentative, between tangles of rose cuttings
And overgrown berry vines, and watch with you
The dimming down behind sun-blackened trellises.

In the halting night, colonies
Of dark follow you toward the light
As the sheen of each new stalk outside
Advances. We put away old arrangements
And I plan our next garden: every row
Will be for you. You lengthen the season.
Where I have rooted there is plenty of time.

## Raspberries Are Not Easily Gotten Rid Of

Raspberries have ways of coming back
years later in fields turned out to pasture
or littered with food wrappers, posts without wires
rotting full-length in wet grass
by the builder's stakes and gravel for the new road.
Sometimes they return at night:
if no one is watching
they grow in wire-brilliant aisles
under a full moon
five stalks per plant, the longest vines
reaching out beyond the row
and bending down to root at the tip,
arch of thorns that will catch each part of you
unawares and hold you there.

Two months after you move to Texas, vines
in ones and twos will cross the hot pavement
of the interstate and root
where rattlers wait for the sun to set,
and spiny three-leaf volunteers will reach
the east bank of the Wabash River in Indiana.
Stocks that grew only between rows
will climb the vandalized fence of the tennis court
in Princeton until the fence is removed.
When the wind kicks up on Lake Champlain
thick vines too old to bear
will catch the main of boats coming about
too close to shore.

More than once raspberries have crossed oceans
as lost luggage. When that happens
Newbergs come as Washingtons,
and Washingtons as Willamettes,
and Willamettes as all-season,
all-weather blight resistant stock
that blooms for years and if cut away
sends up twice as many shoots.

## At the End of the Picking Season

Coolness bursts out of low-branching light
sudden as blossoms, dancing among eyelashes:
morning starved to nakedness by dreams
pendulous as unpicked berries hanging
behind large leaves in the bush's heart,
wires stretched outward bellylike.

This world goes better with eyes open.
I lie in a Swiss-blue bed, hungry
for a hard apple, a yellow-transparent,
and bitter-smooth taste of seeds under tongue,
thinking how our apple trees bend branches down
over themselves and into the outside row
of the raspberry field.  The skylight flames.
Arms etched by a long season reach
out, stinging where berry vines
reached out: *this you must eat.*

Blue flies will be humming in the weighhouse
faint songs of the Panathenaea,
will grow gray repeating them
among departing pickers' voices;
empty berry flats blackened by summer
and stacked whichever way by the roadside,
swaying when the poplars shiver.

I stand, famished, in a stairway of light.

# The Author

Leonard Neufeldt was born and raised in Yarrow, a raspberry-growing hamlet in British Columbia's Fraser Valley. From the 1920s to the 1940s, Yarrow was settled by European Mennonites who had fled the Soviet Union.

Neufeldt received his early education in Yarrow and nearby Chilliwack, followed by a B.A. from Wilfrid Laurier University, and graduate degrees (including a doctorate in English and History) from the University of Illinois. He has taught at the University of Washington, the University of Texas, and at Purdue, where he has remained since 1978.

The author of three books on New England Transcendentalism and one previous book of poetry, Neufeldt has published poems in numerous Canadian and American literary magazines. He is on the editorial team of *The Writings of Henry D. Thoreau* (Princeton University Press), and is a consulting editor for *Humor: International Journal of Humor Research*.

He is married to Mera Louise Klassen of Winnipeg, a medical social worker. They have two daughters and a son.

Upon completing *Raspberrying*, Neufeldt, an avid gardener, plowed under his small berry patch and planted it anew.

Other books by Leonard Neufeldt:

*A Way of Walking* (Fiddlehead Poetry Books, 1972)
*Ralph Waldo Emerson: New Appraisals* (Transcendental Books, 1973)
*The House of Emerson* (University of Nebraska Press, 1982)
*The Economist: Henry Thoreau and Enterprise* (Oxford University Press, 1989)